Merry Christmas

Vintage Pictures and advertising

Retro Books

Presentation

This book consists of a non-systematic series of images to collect, see, and, above all, to use for decoration purposes.

It was designed so that you can detach all images or each one individually, allowing you to frame the pictures you like the most.

The purpose of this book is aesthetic only, to assemble together beautiful images which take us to charming places in the history of great brands of food and drinking products. It is a tribute to so many advertisement creators and label designers that will forever remain in our memories.

For this reason, we do not indicate dates or researches that we made throughout the process of making this book.

Retro Books

CHRISTMAS CHEER.

With kindly Greeting let me say, I think of you this Christmas Day.

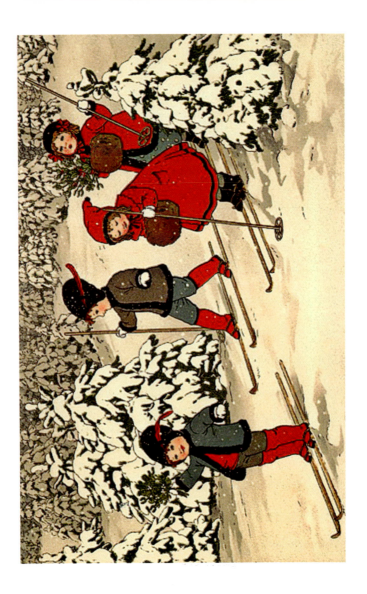

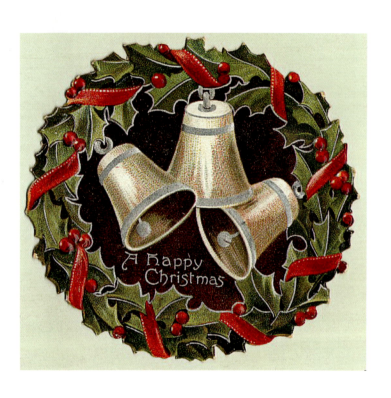

Unit 16 & 17. 12F, Tower A
New Mandarim Plaza,14
Science Museum Rd. TST East
Kowloon, Hong Kong

Printed in Chine